# BLIND DATE
# WITH CAVAFY

# BLIND
# DATE
# WITH
# CAVAFY

poems

*Steve Fellner*

MARSH HAWK PRESS ✦ 2007

for my mother and for Phil

✦

06 07 08 09 10 7 6 5 4 3 2 1 FIRST EDITION

Marsh Hawk Press books are published by Poetry Mailing List, Inc.,
a not-for-profit corporation under section 501 (c) 3 United States
Internal Revenue Code.

Book design, cover and title page photos: Claudia Carlson
The text of this book is Adobe Jenson Pro

Library of Congress Cataloging-in-Publication Data

Fellner, Steve.
  Blind date with Cavafy / Steve Fellner. -- 1st ed.
    p. cm.
  ISBN-13: 978-0-9785555-2-8 (pbk.)
  ISBN-10: 0-9785555-2-X (pbk.)
  I. Title.
  PS3606.E3885B58 2007
  811'.6--dc22

                              2006023344

MARSH HAWK PRESS
P.O. Box 206
East Rockaway, New York 11518-0206
www.marshhawkpress.org

# ACKNOWLEDGEMENTS

The author gratefully acknowledges the editors who have selected the following poems to be included in their magazines.

*Alaska Quarterly*: "Judgment Day"
*American Letters and Commentary*: "The Ghost of Joice Heth on the Truth and the Trees"
*Barrow Street*: "Homosexuality is not a theme"
*Berkeley Poetry Review*: "Blind Date with Cavafy," "Clearing the Air," "Short Cuts"
*can we have our ball back?*: "How I Tried to Banish Self-Insight and Knowledge from My Life and the World"
*Cimarron Review*: "Fun," "Synesthesia"
*Doubletake*: "Desperate Calls"
*Flyway Literary Review*: "The Sterility of Love"
*Greensboro Review*: "Consider the Fates"
*Laurel Review*: "The Ghost of Joice Heth on Fate," "The Ghost of Joice Heth on the Night Before Her Death"
*Mangrove*: "Purity"
*Mid-American Review*: "Miss LaLa," "Upon Discussing Whether We Should Condescend to Science-Fiction Writers"
*Poet Lore*: "Epiphanies," "Miss Bateman's Hen"
*River City*: "Deus Ex Machina"
*Seattle Review*: "God in a Box"
*Spork*: "Self-Portrait"
*32 Poems*: "I Hate You, Too, Catullus"

I would like to thank K.P. Bath, Ralph Black, Ron Christopher, J.D. Dolan, Eric Fellner, Lewis Fellner, Zia Isola, Sophia Kartsonis, Sandy McIntosh, Mother Goose, Anne Panning, Mr. Pokey and the gang, Alicia Preo, Ruby, Samantha Ruckman, Laura Schiller, Andrea Smith, Taffeta, Nicole Walker, Eliot Wilson, Louise Young, and, of course, my beloved Phil E. Young. I'm indebted to the Department of English at SUNY Brockport for their generosity and acceptance of me.

I'd also like to thank Marsh Hawk Press for making my dream come true.

Special thanks to my teachers Robin Hemley, Sandy Huss, David Kranes, Michael Martone, Jacqueline Osherow, Barbara Peiskor, David St. John, Bruce Smith, Kathryn Stockton, Barry Weller, David Wojhan, and most of all, Melanie Rae Thon, who saved me.

# TABLE OF CONTENTS

BLIND DATE
WITH CAVAFY

# Epiphanies

Everyone was having them. You couldn't walk
through the neighborhood streets without seeing people
smacking their foreheads with the palms of their hands,
bragging about another bright idea. Every morning people gossiped
about those who fled their houses during the middle of the night,
leaving their spouses and kids with no better explanation

than carpe diem. By noon all the bars were filled. "Free drinks for everyone,"
someone shouted every couple of minutes, wanting to celebrate
their latest revelation with everybody else. Office supply stores
and card shops couldn't keep journals and diaries in stock
for more than a couple hours. No one dared ask anyone "How are you?"
unless they had an entire afternoon to spare.

I waited for my epiphany. I tried to be patient. Would it hit me
like a bolt of lightning, striking my skull with such force
I could be laid up in a recovery ward for months?
Or would it sneak up on me like a pinprick? Something I might
not even notice if I was too busy reveling in everybody else's revelations?
Would an epiphany be more likely to enter a quiet house

or descend upon a rowdy block party? A peaceful meadow
or busy shopping mall? Would it offer its wisdom in the form
of a direct statement or a cagey rhetorical question?
Could one have multiple epiphanies, one right after the other?
Or does it offer its news in distinct, evenly spaced installments?
Would it want me to lavish praise upon its presence like Zoloft or Prozac?

Or would it prefer to go unnoticed, unmentioned like your mother's advice
you take for granted? And what happens when the moment is over,
the life changed? Does the epiphany disappear from the mind
like memorized facts from history books? Or does it reincarnate itself
into the suddenly remembered final digit of a telephone number?
Or the long-forgotten name of an acquaintance who never stopped
    thinking of you?

# Miss La La

Seeing you, Miss LaLa, black
woman acrobat,
hanging from a thin rope
by your teeth
in the dome
of the Cirque Fernando,
makes me ashamed I crave
the world's attention for doing
nothing. In Degas' sketches, you never once look
down at him. He loves mammies more
than your bare legs and mop of dark hair,
according to his diary. He respects you
enough to reveal your fascination
with the ceiling. How many times did you pound
your fists against the top of the dome and hope
the angels would hear your knock
and unleash the heavens into the ring. Maybe
it's a good thing
the otherworldly keeps its distance.
Who could guarantee
you wouldn't shriek
and then, of course, fall? Once I stared
at your picture so long, the rope
vanished. Gravity refused
to abandon you. You danced alone in the shallow sky.
Degas never once sketched the audience.
Who undoubtedly clenched their own teeth
and prayed. Their gasps float to the top of the dome
and offer themselves to you
as handfuls of useless, benign air.

# DESPERATE CALLS

The summer I turned seventeen I worked
for a bill collection agency. Hiding
in the far back corner of the office,

I whispered wishy-washy threats to people,
my voice lower than the most muted elevator music.
I reminded someone with a thick Russian accent

to seal the envelope, so the check wouldn't slip
away again. Mother had stopped drinking.
Once after I crept inside our house, I saw

her sitting Indian style in front of the empty liquor cabinet.
She was muttering to herself. I couldn't understand
her words. Unlike the Russian who said her child

died and "funerals cost money," I couldn't tell
mother to slow down, articulate. She pantomimed
a wine glass and then brought its rim to her lips.

She offered to pour me a glass. "No," I said. I drank
straight from the bottle, swishing the invisible liquid
inside my mouth, never wanting to forget the taste

of nothing. Two desks to my right was Jack, a bald-headed,
bearded man who was always clearing his throat. Whenever
someone swore, he hung up. I never disconnected.

Once after a man called him a cocksucker and threatened
to bomb the building, Jack set down the phone and strutted
out of the office. I picked up the phone and heard tears,

the same ones mother shed in the locked bathroom
after we forced our burps and pretended to stagger
drunkenly around the apartment, promising

that this was the last time. Cold turkey.
We swore. I imagined Jack sitting on the bathroom toilet,
his trousers around his ankles, hitting his head

lightly against the wall. "Send the check," I said
to the client on the line and then added, "Please."
He promised it wouldn't be more than two days.

FedEx. Swear to Christ. You've got my word.

# Upon Discussing Whether We Should Condescend to Science-Fiction Writers

Let's pretend we really believe fanged anorexic midget space aliens want to
    rape our pets
and turn The President of the United States
into soggy cotton candy. Let's pretend otherworldly creatures want
to trash our souls, take our bodies, and dance a mamba.
Let's pretend all extraterrestrials look like a perfect cross
between us and roadkill. Except shorter and with fatter heads.
Let's pretend monsters from other universes want to burn Planet Earth
to ashes so they can fertilize their craters.
Let's pretend they want to know everything about us. Like how it feels to fart
and breathe and skid on our knees and why we fall in love with humans
who look just like us yet strangely never love us back. Let's pretend we'll take
    their advice
and give our hearts to plants and vegetables
and ice cream sundaes and icebergs. Things that will never abandon us. Or at
    least not today.
Let's pretend there's not enough in this world to write about.
Let's pretend that on other planets seeing the end of infinity
is even more common than winning $37,687,324.90 in the state lottery. Except
you expect it to happen every other day.
Let's pretend our planet is an exciting place.
Where we don't feel the need to search for the few interesting people
in the universe. Like the man who has the body of a sumo wrestler
and the face of Little Orphan Annie. He works
at the convenience store down the block. His name is Arnie.
Let's pretend we don't feel the compulsion to steal
the newest set of encyclopedias from the public library, binging on the latest facts.
Let's pretend we make friends because we want good conversation,
a free meal every so often. Not because we want to see them
sob in front of us at some point in the future.
Let's pretend the human soul is more complicated than the alphabet.
And that the planets and the moon and the sun and the asteroids and all the
    other galaxies
in the Universe are a popcorn trail, leading us to the heart of God.

# Short Cuts

The winter after your death
I freelanced
for *CliffsNotes*, tightening

already tight plot summaries
for famous,
boring novels. College undergrads

wrote those study guide masters
letters
more impassioned than anything

they'd scribble to their own families
or lovers:
"Even with your invaluable help,

*Remembrance of Things Past*
is a bigger challenge
than tracing all the storylines

from the last two years of *The Young
and the Restless*.
I almost feel I need to read

certain passages more than once.
I swore I'd rescue
students from the torture

of sorting out Hamlet's needless
ambiguities, seeing
the welts from Dimmesdale's

self-flagellation, surveying
the duller points
in Dante's tour of hell. Weeks before

you left this world, you gave away
your Dolly Parton albums,
high school track trophies, lucky

pair of glow-in-the-dark shoelaces,
Menudo and Marky
Mark posters, cock rings, unicycle, "Don't Tell

Anyone I'm Gay" t-shirt, lava lamp,
fake refund receipts
from the Gap, and the plastic pink

wading pool. I saved the answering machine
cassette
with the first message you left, erasing

any other voices with the steady silence
of my grief.
Every night for months I listened

to you say, "Pick up the phone, you jerk!
Your books will always
be there." After a few months

I obliterated everything
except "you jerk"
and transferred it onto a regular tape,

playing it in my car whenever I left
my house to visit the forest
preserve. Where gay men in cars circled

around the watertower, looking
for a pretty young face.
Once someone asked my name.

"Let's skip the foreplay," I said.
I rushed
home and worked for hours. Still horny,

I paged through original Shakespeare plays,
drawing lines through any lines
failing to advance the plot. I remembered

when we squirmed through a college
production of *The Winter's Tale.*
You snored during the King's monologues

of sexual jealousy and grief. When I pinched
your love handles,
you jumped and wanted me to say

you didn't miss the part where the wild
bear chases Antigonus.
Weeks ago I abbreviated that scene

to a mere phrase, a present participle,
nothing larger
than the smallest of footnotes.

When I complained to you about having
to read
*Crime and Punishment* for the survey course

I taught, you said, "Skim the last hundred
pages. Endings
never surprise." You knew you would die

once your suicide note felt right,
unrevisable:
*Sorry about the mess.*

# BREAKFAST WITH SOCRATES

I bet Socrates hated waking up in the morning.
With every sip of coffee, he thought about the possibility
of choking, which led him to ponder the afterlife,
the meaning of his life, our lives. Never being able to leave
his work at the office must have annoyed him. Why think
deep thoughts if you're not clocked in, if no one's tallying
the leaps of your mind? No doubt his wife Xanthippe
counted the number of nights he came home
without any money, the times he changed
the conversation from finances to the danger
of living life without the fear of God.
I bet she craved the art of small talk. How horrible
to threaten divorce and receive a litany
of reasons as to how betrayal is an essential
and necessary component in any relationship.
No doubt she overheard him repeat his words
to his best friend Chaerephon. "Quicken your pace.
Devise a clearer outline of your main points," he said.
Socrates took his advice. His speech became
his Monday lecture for his students. He reached
his thesis a full two minutes earlier. Weeks later
she wondered, "Does he forget to feed the cat
and take out the garbage on purpose?
Does he hope a fight will inspire his next keynote address?"
She never told him he did his best work sleeping.
Every night he mumbled about Justice, Goodness,
and his secret stage fright. If she admitted
to eavesdropping, he'd make her stay up, record every word,
even the slightest of snores. Always waking up
a full hour before him, she made his coffee,
and joked his obsessive need to think
was nothing more than a result of too much caffeine.
They forced their laughter, each praying
something else would be released
in their desperate, knowing noise.

# PURITY

*In the late 18th century, an African-American man who went*
*simply by the name Wilson modeled for many white artists.*

As Hayden built a wall around my naked
      black body & poured
         in seven bushels

of plaster, he told me to relax. How many times
      did I & other models laugh
         about the shaky hands of white

artists? Straight lines were as endangered
      as colored men.
         When the dead white

cast began to harden & my breaths
      grew shorter, I told him
         about the black man

who strangled a painter
      for making him more
         beautiful than God.

In his diaries, he contemplated renting me to George Dawe,
      who wanted to draw me wrestling
         a buffalo. Unlike Hayden,

he wanted my every muscle extended.
      "How does it feel to be so still?"
         he asked a moment

before I nearly moaned. I decided to keep
      quiet. You never master
         motion. Which is

as overrated & duplicitous
        as finished art.
                If, as Hayden said, my mold

has "the purity of a seashell," the music inside
        sounds more like his heartbeat
                than the ocean.

# God in a Box

Everyone gave me money to sneak a peek
at God. My grade school friends
wanted to look through the slits
of my cigar box which contained
His elbow, surrounded by three
ladybugs. They were His bodyguards.
To claim I captured anything more
than a limb of the Lord seemed odd.
Surely God was bigger and swifter
than the fireflies we smashed
with our puny fists. I charged a quarter
for a five second look. All the kids
handed over part of their lunch
money. Some their lunch.
No one was disappointed
with what they saw. My best friend
stole a five dollar bill from his
mother's purse so he could have
the box for a night. A kid who lived
three houses down from mine claimed
he captured a strand of God's hair.
It was bright yellow and twelve inches long.
He charged one whole dollar.
Soon everybody claimed they had
part of God's body: earlobe, thigh,
lower intestine, pancreas, spleen,
toenail. Someone tried to charge
a dollar for a look at His navel. I left
letters on all my friends' and enemies'
front door steps, asking them
to come to my backyard and bring
whatever part of God they had.
We stood in a circle and named
the limbs and organs. All
together we had enough

for almost three full corpses.
I threw my box into the air
and watched His elbow
soar toward the heavens.
Cans, boxes, thermoses and pails
littered the sky. That night
we went back to sneaking up
on fireflies, surprising them
with our tenacity
as they surprised us
with their weak humble light.

# MISS BATEMAN'S HEN

*In the autumn of 1806 in a tavern in Leeds, England,*
*Mary Bateman's hen started laying eggs inscribed with*
*the words "Christ is Coming."*

You couldn't tell that the hen
was about to give birth
to the end of the world.
It was perched on top
of a barstool, its back turned
to the three hundred people
gathered to see her lay
the fourteenth and final egg.
Eight months pregnant
with my sixth child,
I pushed my way
through the crowd
and knelt in front of the hen.
I reached to pluck
one of its tail feathers.
Miss Bateman grabbed my arm
and threatened to call
the police. How could she blame
me for wanting to touch
death? Who doesn't want
a small part of it? For the first time
I wanted my children
next to me. I wanted to see them
flap their arms, jump up
and down, shake their butts.
I wanted them to peck
my face with their lips.
For the first time I wanted
to go back home and explain
that I needed to abandon them
to see the hen cluck and shudder

moments before it released
our doom. I wanted
to feel those sympathy
pains. I wanted to swoon and sink
to the ground. I wanted to announce
to the world that the end
always comes again.

# DEUS EX MACHINA

Our high school English teacher took out her cigarette
lighter and set her copy of *A Winter's Tale* in flames after we read
the part where Herimone becomes human and happy again
after suffering temporarily as a marble statue. "When art lies,"
she said, "it must pay the price or we do." We all heard rumors
about Mrs. Beerbohm refusing to talk to her sister
once she won over a million dollars in the Illinois State Lottery
and decided to take an early retirement
as a phone receptionist. A day after someone asked if it was true,
Mrs. Beerbohm showed us the *Daily Herald* photo
with her sister holding up the winning ticket. "Deus ex machina,"
she said and cursed her sister's name, tearing the picture
into little pieces, giving every student a piece. Twenty-four years later
and I still carry mine in my wallet behind the photos
of my parents, normal people who would have been relieved
that Shakespeare gave that misunderstood wife
a second chance at mortality. If I challenged them,
repeating that Latin phrase, they would have laughed. Like I do
when I read stories in the paper about a celebrity who meets an ordinary
waitress and rescues her from a life of refilling people's coffee cups.
There have been times in my life I wanted to douse my apartment
furniture in gasoline and light a match. But then I read
the Want Ads and decide to change jobs for the third time
in a month. Soon the company decides to make us
pay for our own life insurance or shortens
our lunch break to half an hour. I end up having to buy small things
to make myself happy. Knickknacks for the ledge
above my fireplace. A vase. A small, dumb statue
I imagine a man made of his lover
days before he found on his kitchen table a note that read:
*Sorry but something came up and I have the once in a lifetime*
*chance to change my life and make my life an unexpected*
*fairy tale.* He wasn't surprised by her exit. Only that she imagined
she couldn't alter her life before this "chance." He read the note
several hundred times, hoping to discover what it was.

# In Honor of the Chinese Poet Li Po

How wrong to assume
Li Po was depressed
and wanted to kill himself
when he stepped
out of his boat in the middle
of a river, half-drunk
on cheap red wine and fully aware
he couldn't swim. He tried
to kiss and embrace the reflection
of the moon in the water,
as the legend says. Only a poet
scolds young children for not jumping
high enough into the air
to touch the moon. "Try again," he shouts.
If the children seem satisfied
when their fingers graze the belly
of a seagull, he yells, "Don't stop. Jump
higher." Why should people consider the moon
as distant as a much sought after line
of poetry? The sky wants more
attention than kind, perfunctory words
on a starry night. Simple observation
can be a dangerous thing. You begin
to forget the moon offers its image
for reasons other than to be studied.
It wants to trick itself into believing
the distance between the earth and the sky
is nothing more than the blink of human eyes.

# FUN

Memoirists rarely write about it.
Most people never remark on its presence
if it's present. Too busy opening birthday presents
or licking the cheese from their fingers.
Someone eventually asks the cruelest question
in a game of Truth or Dare:
"When was the last time you had fun?"
Everyone's waiting for you to answer. You don't remember
the night when you and mother guzzled plum wine
on your Prom night and then egged
your ex-girlfriend's house. Nor do you recall
having a seizure in the middle of a Van Gogh exhibit.
The idea of your writhing body upstaging
those precious wheatfields amused you
for months. You do remember that you laughed
real hard a few months ago over some dumb joke about a goat
and a priest. But that doesn't seem fun
enough somehow, at least nothing to make
the newlyweds at the party regret their impulsive vows.
You won't mention anything to do with amusement parks,
carnivals, discos, costume and Tupperware parties,
Bingo night, renaissance fairs. Hordes of festive people
have always made you nervous. The aftermath
of small crises loosens you up, like the time your ex-lover
left a message on your answering machine:
"I'm pregnant. You may be the father. Call me
if you want to know." You called her back.
She confessed the bad news was a lie:
she bought a beagle and wanted to share
the good news with someone. You bought
yourself a $100 savings bond to celebrate
your newly felt freedom. You had never felt better
unless you count the moments after your oncologist
told you that the CATscan revealed you're not suffering
from the brain tumor he was convinced was there.

Those were the days... You snap
out of your trance when someone repeats the question:
"When was the last time you had fun?"
Everyone's waiting for you to name the thing
they never knew they craved. What else can you do
but withhold your reply for another moment?
Their faces shine with gratitude.

# The Concept of the External Soul

The one inside me never makes enough
noise. No matter how much pain
fills my day, it never slithers from the bottom
of my stomach, up my esophagus, and out
my mouth. How I wish it would escape,
belching and yodeling,
doing cartwheels and oozing
green pus. Or whatever divine things
are supposed to do when they enter
another world. Sometimes I forget
it's even in there, undoubtedly perched
on my large intestine, bored of the sight
of my internal organs pumping and beating
in their unflamboyant ways. How I wish
I knew how my soul is responding to my
writing a poem about its presence
in my body, constructing it
as if it were another one of my unremarkable
friends. Or maybe I'm glad I don't. What if
the soul is nothing special: an overhyped mood ring
which records the predictable movements
of our minds, flashing from color to color
in a pattern as predictable
as a stoplight? Let's prove
that theory wrong and emulate
the King of Ceylon from India
who could transport his soul
from his body into a box
while he went to war. Did his soul
elongate to at least three times its normal size
when released into the open air?
Did it squawk and kick the sides
of its prison? Or did it nestle itself
into a corner and try to reach the ceiling,
mistaking it for Heaven? How typical

for a nervous human to imagine
the soul as some cuddly creature. Something
that could easily be replaced
by another bothersome pet. What if
the soul resembles nothing more
than a piece of dust
when it exits our dead body? Our lover
unknowingly sweeps it
into a garbage bag. We become our own gods
without even knowing it.

# JUDGMENT DAY

The line is long. Hundreds
of millions of people are waiting
to reach the end where God gives
them the once over and a slip of paper.
Everyone is kind. Eerily polite. They all
encourage you to go before them. A woman three
hundred spots ahead of you offers
to switch places. You shake your head
and say, "No thanks. I like where I am."
The line stretches across several
continents. Angels hover above you,
offering crossword puzzle books, cigarettes,
Dixie cups of red wine, fraudulent smiles.
You make small talk with the man behind you.
He has a thick Russian accent. He tells
you about the lines in the Soviet Union
where everyone hopes the person in front
of them drops dead so they can take
their spot and maybe get an extra loaf
of bread and roll of toilet paper.
You laugh. The angels hush you.
Everyone in the world stops moving.
You hear God tapping his fingers
on a large desk. The sound reminds you
of thunderbolts. "God needs silence,"
an angel says. "He doesn't want to send
a good soul to Hell by accident."
When someone faints, an angel dumps
cold water on their face. When someone claims
they can't stand any longer, the angels bring
a wheelchair. Everyone has to keep moving.
You wonder how God can listen to everyone's litany
of sins without yawning. When you get closer to Him,
you hear people mumbling their sins, rehearsing
to themselves. He doesn't want

any stumbles. When you find yourself
in front of Him, you notice He doesn't look
at you. He looks around you.
His gaze takes in the line which still wraps
around Australia, North America,
and The Philippine Islands.
He blinks, fearful that when He opens
His eyes, He won't see an end.

# Capgras Delusion

*"...describes individuals who are disturbed by the firm belief that family, friends, and/or items of personal significance have been replaced by copies or impersonating doubles."*
—*Louis R. Franzini, Ph.D. and John Grossberg, Ph.D.*

When I was seven, *Invasion of the Body Snatchers*
made me pee in my pants. What could be more

terrifying than space aliens murdering your mother
and father and pet dog during their sleep

only to replace them with soulless replicants
who shuffle around the house? Until they discover

you haven't been replaced by some half-wit pod person.
Which causes them to scream and try to stab you

with syringes loaded with super strong sedatives.
Now I realize my belief that *BS* was a horror film

is BS. It was God's instruction manual. Which somehow fell
from the sky into the hands of humans. Not even God

can reinvent the world in one move. Projects like that
take time. Not to mention He has a heart. To lose

one friend or relative is devastating enough. But a hundred
million. The world can only sustain so much grief.

He takes us one at a time, leaving substitutes
in our wakes. How many times have I fallen

asleep, and dreamed that hanging from every stoplight
would be TV screens showing a colorized

*It's a Wonderful Life.* People would realize
life is better than wonderful when you can see cheeks

blush, navy blue suits, and the dark look of terror
in Jimmy Stewart's eyes. God could no longer dangle

the Platonic ideal in front of our noses like a ball
of string and wait for us to jump, trying to claw

some stupid prize. Too bad we don't win anything
when He decides to replace us with something

less free and feisty. No badly stitched teddy bears
for our souls to hold when He decides to lock

them up in a safe on a nondescript comet
somewhere between Pluto and Hell,

and then hurries His monsters to seize
the rest of our bodies. While empty-headed aliens

try to vote one of their own as President
in order to pass a federal law

saying everybody must nap,
I will remember a memory I never had:

opening night of a Broadway revival of King Lear.
The entire cast stricken with mono. The director hired

only one understudy. Who was forced to perform
all the characters himself. He sat on a wooden chair

in the middle of the stage. And did it. Afterwards
he locked himself in his dressing room and talked

to himself. The echo of his own voice soothed him.

# "Homosexuality is not a theme"

I scrawl on an essay about Walt Whitman's poetry by my favorite student Jeremy who happens to be openly gay and who sits in the far right hand corner in order to receive a perfect view of the room when I announce my homosexuality to a class full of teenagers skilled enough to read me as a queer through my enigmatic love of words and well-ironed clothes, yet they unequivocally believe the narrator in Adrienne Rich's "Twenty-One Love Poems" to be straight. Jeremy waits for me to put an end to everybody's questions. Solve the puzzle for them. No one's told him I'm gay, I suppose. Probably figured he already knew. He was in Wyoming for a funeral the day I came out. A student turned to his classmate and whispered, "Did our teacher just tell us he's a cocksucker?" accompanied by an audible gagging noise. That was the extent of the discrimination. I thought it'd be a bigger deal. Almost disappointed there wasn't more drama. One female student told me in an individual conference her sister loves homosexuals. She calls them her "pets." No offense was taken. That's how I feel about my students and most of the human race: pets. Jeremy never does linger after class to ask me questions about any of the poems carefully selected for English 103: Introduction to Poetry. He rushes out the door and fails to visit me during my office hours to chat. True. I'm never there. But I have things to say to him. Nothing about poetry, of course. But I do want to make some things clear. As an undergraduate, I guessed the narrator of "Twenty-One Love Poems" was queer by the end of sonnet twelve: "we were two lovers of one gender..." How proud I was to have been the only one to figure it out. When my high school English teacher Mr. Jacobs found out some of us read Whitman in junior high, he called the teacher immoral and then said, "No one should read Whitman at that age. Too ambiguous for young minds. They'll be put off and never read it again." Mr. Jacobs was an unhappily married man. In front of him and my peers, I confessed to loving Whitman and thanked my junior high school teacher for the introduction. I didn't understand a word of Whitman back then. But it didn't matter. It was Literature. It was like the time when I was seven and Mother confided in me. After drinking half a bottle of wine and smoking two joints, she confessed that Father treated her like furniture and she was happiest in her marriage when he left us to stay in the hospital after suffering a stroke. Mr. Jacobs took me after class and said I was an "exception." "A cut above the rest," he said. He hugged me and then started to cry. I put my arms around his belly and he hugged me back. I lied to the school psychologist, saying that Mr. Jacobs put his hand down my pants. He feigned shock. The next year Mr. Jacobs never came back. We all pretended we didn't know why. Every day for eight years, I pined for him. On the third day of class, Jeremy raised his hand and asked the class why we all assumed Shakespeare was writing his love sonnets to a woman. You could tell he thought it was a brilliant deduction. Something you'd expect from a private eye. His classmates were unimpressed. As if they, too, read the ending to the same mystery novel. Sometimes I think my students would be more interested in surveying mystery novels than poetry. Poetry makes them agitated and sleepy and horny. Everyone likes a good mystery. Everyone likes to be surprised by what they already know. Teaching students to write about poetry is like trying to bring your victim back to life after you spiked the drink, suffocated him with a pillow, dismembered the arms and legs, tossed the torso in a ditch. Feel free to leave as many clues as you want. Be as careless as you desire. Go ahead drop the chainsaw. Don't bother wiping off your fingerprints. Everything's a red herring. No one will learn a thing.

# I Hate You, Too, Catullus

When a student saw me perusing a poem of yours in the original Latin,
I bet he thought that I was some dumb undergraduate
who couldn't roll his r's in Spanish and was using you
to fulfill my foreign language requirement. Not that I like to speak a
    lot or write much.
That's why I choose to emulate you, a poet of fragments, a poet perfect
for those of us who have short attention spans, who find more comfort
from glossy magazines and backs of cereal boxes than sweet elegies
about someone's dead brother who cheated on his wife with someone
who wasn't as attractive as her. Not that that's necessarily a bad thing.
When I carry around your book, I am happy
that it is a book by a dead man, a man who will never utter another
    word again,
who will not be able to scold me for ripping off his verse
as a way to gain the love and attention I don't know how to get on my
    own.
Let me tell you dead man: I am worse than a grave robber.
I am worse than the dirt that caresses your bones. I am worse
than the gravestone that is so conceited over the fact it designates the
    place
where genius will rest for an eternity. Oh yes, I am worse than all that
because I won't get my hands dirty when I turn the pages
of your volume smudged by the fingerprints
of thousands of young students so unclean
in their mindless appreciation of you.
I run to the nearest sink and wash the love away.

# Listen to Me, Catullus, and Listen to Me Good, This is the Truth

You said lesbia was proof
a benevolent god existed.

Don't be so naïve, Catullus:
all love goes badly so accept

miracles are nothing
more than accidents we like.

# SELF-PORTRAIT

My adoptive mother is all teeth
and hair.
    Buck teeth, red frizzy hair. Her name is Winnie.

I met my birth mother

in the parking lot of a Pizza Hut.
She told me she'd be wearing a baseball cap
and a legbrace. Her name:
Maxine. Winnie insisted

    she come along.

  ("Moral support," she said.)

On the way there, she asked me
Maxine's name three times.

Maxine drove up in a Yellow Cab.
"Just got off my shift," she said,
    "I love my job. You never know

who's going to end up in your back seat.
Yesterday it was Tom Hanks.
Two months ago Tom Selleck.
    Who knows who's next?"

    My growling stomach broke the silence.

The first thing Winnie said to Maxine:
    "We look so much alike." It was true.

They could have passed
for sisters.

◆ ◆ ◆

Winnie hid it somewhere.
I was convinced.

My umbilical cord was nowhere
　　　　　　　　to be found. First place

I checked: her oak dresser
drawers. A half-empty plastic bag
of hashish, a fake gold locket with no
picture inside,　yellowing letters from a man
who spelled love luv
and dotted his i's
　　　　　　with hearts,
　　　　　　　　　　my baby teeth glued on cardboard.
I ran down the steep stairs.

She didn't hear me. She was vacuuming
the attic.　I whipped
kitchen cabinet after kitchen cabinet
　　　　　　　　　wide open, shoved my hand
　　　　　　　　　down the garbage disposal, stuck
　　　　　　　　　my head in the oven.

Underneath the plaid couch covered in plastic:
no luck. When I looked up, my mother stood
on the landing.
　　　　　　She waved a white
　　　　　　　　　cashmere scarf, lassoing

　　　　my leg, and then pulled me close to her body.

I stood on her naked feet.

After I tied a knot around our bodies,
we danced a slow dance. The scarf

fell to the floor. This dream
haunted me for eight consecutive nights in college.

So on the ninth, I took
a sleeping pill,

because someone told me you don't dream
under its influence. And then I took another

for no reason.

They worked. But when I woke up and walked into my living room,
all my furniture was rearranged: the couch

propped against the bathroom door; the glass cover
to my kitchen table laid
on the folding lawn chair in the patio;
my computer was unplugged, repackaged

in its original box; the jigsaw puzzle
I finished two days prior

disassembled, scattered

like confetti all over the bathtub.

My mind fell asleep. My body
resisted. Later that morning,
I walked outside and saw

a homeless person flipping through a photo album. I recognized
my mother's handwriting
on the cover. So I said, "Excuse me?
Where did you find
that?" She threw it

into the dumpster and ran.

♦ ♦ ♦

Homosexuality is my choice. I wanted
childlessness.

♦ ♦ ♦

Once I had sex with a woman. I already knew
I was gay. She knew I was gay. But
we were bored.

She was obsessed with a man
                    who tattooed the name Belinda
                    on his arm.
Belinda was the name of his mother.
"I insist we have sex in the dark," she told me.

As we kissed, the phone rang.
The answering machine turned on,
                            but once she heard him
                            scream, "You bitch.
I need you more than I need

my own mother," she stopped, asked me
to leave the room
and argued with him for a full two hours.
                        Several weeks later we found
ourselves bored again. She didn't want me

to use a condom. "What if you get pregnant?" I said.

"I'll lie and tell him it's his," she said.

♦ ♦ ♦

Once Winnie and I attended
a National Honors Society Banquet.
My friends and we ate Sloppy Joes
and cheesebread in the cafeteria
                         with our teachers.
No one had anything to say

except someone's mother who praised
the Sloppy Joes for their "remarkable consistency."

Eventually, someone else remarked
the hallways were a nice yellow.
                    Winnie told everyone
                    about her Cesarean section:
                    how my younger brother came out
with his thumb in his mouth.
(Doctors told her
no children in her future.
Her psychic confirmed this,
so she searched for me.
Everyone told her later
my brother is a godsend.)

              "He sucks it to this very day," she boasted.

Someone asked about my birth:
"Anything weird there?"
Winnie told her I was adopted.
              "Nothing too strange.

              No birth defects
              as you can see.

After all, he made it here."
              The parents didn't know what to say,

so they clapped and cheered.

◆ ◆ ◆

I saw *A Nightmare On Elm Street*
in a completely empty theatre
                            on the Fourth of July.

(Only orphans and widows go
to the movies on national holidays.)
Dressed in a tattered black and red sweater,

a guy named Freddy with third-degree burns

engraves his name on the faces
                            of good-looking teens
                            who have nothing better to do

than die.

In one scene, old Freddy appears
out of nowhere

and chases a woman with huge breasts
into a furnace room.
                    I peed in my pants
and sat in my urine, because I didn't want
to miss him
slashing her body. Before he shoved
                            his nails into her stomach,
he said, "I'm the bastard
                    son of a thousand maniacs!"

◆ ◆ ◆

On Thursdays, Winnie and I shopped
for groceries. While she zoomed her cart through the aisles,

I stalked single middle-aged women.

I was seven at the time.

                      Once I seized
a pregnant woman's leg. She kicked me
and screamed for help. Winnie rushed

into the aisle and pulled
my hair until I let go.


"He's not mine," Winnie told her.

        ❖ ❖ ❖


I discovered photos of two teenage kids
in my lover's wallet. He was 53. I was

17. Were they his other
boyfriends? I swore I saw their faces

on the backs of milk cartons and missing posters.

               *Lucky bastards,* I thought,
                          *Someone's looking*

for you. One afternoon he said, "My wife needs
me to take care of my children
for the weekend. Would you like to help?"

                    "Let me think about it," I said.
That same night I snuck out of our bed

and scrawled a note and then taped it
next to my college report cards  (all A's)
on his refrigerator door.

It said: "There's not enough room
in anybody's life for two babies. Never
contact me again." He called.
Which was more

        than my father ever did

after he deserted us
for another woman,
two days after they received
me from the agency.

      *She needs me,*

            he wrote on a postcard from Los Angeles.
            *You two have each other.*

My father was right. On my answering machine,
Willis sobbed. "I dropped them
          off at the movies. Found a baby sitter.
Come back, kiddo."
            That same night I showed up at his apartment.

"Promise you'll give me
a good beating," I said.

       ✦ ✦ ✦

I have another best friend who is a woman.
She is fifty and talks a little funny.
Encephalitis. Ex-heroin addict.
"A Buddhist told me

            my soul has outgrown

this body," she said. When we watch
movies together, she excuses herself
to go the bathroom and sniffs

Elmer's Glue.

I asked her if she's ever had an abortion.

               "Are you kidding?" she said,
               "Of course." How many?
               She started to count her fingers
and then stopped.
        "Do you want me to round up
or down?"

               "Maybe I'm one of the aborted babies

reincarnated," I said. She laughed

and then slapped me.

      ◆ ◆ ◆

Before my junior high dance, I confessed
to Winnie that I never kissed a girl.
"Do you want to practice
               on me?" she said. I stood
               on my toes and shut my eyes,
puckering my lips. Her lips
were cold. She smelled like beer
and Noxzema. The kiss lasted
               a millisecond. "Maybe you should try

               this on your pillow," she said.

      ◆ ◆ ◆

I talked to Maxine only one other time.

I called her from college long-distance.
She regurgitated headlines from the tabloids

about famous movie stars:  HARRISON FORD

ARRESTED FOR BIGAMY, ROSEANNE BARR

PREGNANT WITH THE POPE'S CHILD. She cooed

when she said their names.
She was used to loving people

                            from a distance, I suppose.
"Are you gay?" she asked, "Don't lie.
I read *The Enquirer.* I know
what's out there." I sighed:
"I don't know."
                         It was a good enough response
                         to keep her on the line

for another twenty minutes.

"I'm not great
at small talk," she said.
And then added:
                       "I almost forgot. I always
skip the major things.
A month after we met
you won't believe who
called... My other son."

                       "A brother?" I said.
She laughed so hard
                       she sounded like a laugh track
gone berserk. "I put
eight kids up
for adoption
during my life. Each
from a different guy. Two
contacted me before you.

41

Four down, four
to go."

I banged the receiver against the wall
and shouted, "Do you hear that?
                    I think
                            there's a bad connection."

And then I hung up and screened my messages
for a year. Just in case.

She never did.

              ✦ ✦ ✦

My undergraduate history teacher forgot
our names.

        Alzheimer's. On Tuesdays
he called me Sunny, on Thursdays
Duke. On the final, we all missed

                    Question Number Fifteen. He gave us

the wrong dates for the Spanish Civil War.
So everyone got a freebie. Two years later
I took a political science class. The teacher asked

if anyone knew when the Spanish Civil War began.

Without thinking, I raised my hand and offered
the wrong date: 1926. I never learned
the right one. Everyone wrote down

my inaccuracy. No one questioned it.
This memory has stopped
me from killing myself

on at least nine different occasions.

＊ ＊ ＊

I've always had two birthdays.
One on the day I was born,
July 18, the other on the day
                    I was adopted, November 2.
I once lied to my grade school teacher
and told her my birthday
                    was the latter, because otherwise

no party for me: my real birthday
landed in the summer: school
was out of session.

                    My mother threw two parties.
In high school, I rebelled
                    against her: After she grounded me for sneaking
                    out of the house after midnight, I confessed
that I "sucked

        the homecoming king's cock

                            and he enjoyed it
more than me." I refused
to attend my second birthday party that year.

"We'll do it without you," Winnie said.

And she did.

I hold her in the highest respect for that.

All my friends and relatives were there.
Naked, I locked myself in the upstairs bathroom
with two joints and jerked off.

I slid into my sweatpants
and crept down the stairs. Everyone was circled

around the cake on the living room table.

The lights were shut off.

They were singing "Happy Birthday to You."
I walked into the room.
"Glad you're here," she said,
"But I should have figured.
                    You always make an entrance."

I didn't tell her I feel that pressure every day.

They started the song from the beginning.
Winnie and I stood in front of the cake.

I let her blow out the candles.
She tried so hard
                to blow them out all at once
you could see her spit
on the tips of eight candles.

The room was so dark
she whispered, "Honey,
are you there? Give me
your hand."

I didn't move. I didn't say anything.
And then someone turned on the lights.

# THE STERILITY OF LOVE

For fun we flossed our teeth
and pressed our ears against the bathroom wall and waited
for the neighbors to duel death threats. They never did.
They were a nice couple. Jane and Mark. As nice
and lean as their abbreviated names. On the first day we moved
into the complex, they made us an inoffensive
meat loaf and tepid strawberry wine. That didn't stop us
from calling the police on them weeks later. We heard something.
Nothing audible. Like the opera albums the single woman
underneath us plays ever since her hip operation. Nothing
like that. But it was something. Which could lead
to something else. Picture the man who dissects his taco salad
with the precision of a neurosurgeon and finds
a hair. Of course, it's his own. But still.
It's there. He almost ate it.

# THE GHOST OF JOICE HETH ON FATE

*Joice Heth was P.T. Barnum's first act. She claimed
to be the 165-year-old mammy of George Washington.*

Perhaps when the Fates spun my thread
It flew from their fingers
Landing in a place too far from their reach

Forcing them to abandon a life

How I yearned to hear the scissors cut
The insidiously knotted string of my life
I always made an effort to visit the costume lady

Talking to her for what felt like an eternity

Her sewing needle dove into the finest fabrics
With a grace only another mother could love
I noticed I always took a deep breath

When it was time for her to cut the thread

I remember the story of her making a rainbow-
Colored quilt for the baby who was supposed to die
In her womb yet managed to see daylight

And continued to breathe for as long as I knew her

Six months pregnant she swore to everyone
The baby had stopped kicking, something was wrong
Doctors prescribed medicines that did nothing

So she refused to touch the spool of thread for that quilt

Thinking the Fates may have wanted her to do their dirty work
She hid all the remnants in a trunk packed in her attic
And making nothing in its place, offering her child

Only the warmth of her own body and breath

Whenever she thought to finish that quilt she sewed jewels
Onto the sleeves of Jenny Lind's already bespectacled dresses
Or started to create something for my next birthday

Something with seams so perfect

I spent countless nights unearthing
Those threads with my long dirty fingernails
That looked like they came from a body

Just released from its own grave

# The Ghost of Joice Heth on the Night Before Her Death

My dying wish was honored
A fortune teller sat at my bedside and predicted

My past which was not easy to do
Considering I had so many of them

My caretaker had joked he might want to bring
A magnifying glass since the lines

On my palms were so wrinkled and deep
When he traced them I started to giggle

Which scared him, I think, because he was afraid
Of what would happen when I stopped

He offered me no specific past events of my lives
Except to say things began awhile ago

And haven't ended yet
Then he continued to stroke that line

That stretched across my palm so shamelessly
And begged to be massaged from time to time

I put my hand on his shoulder and whispered
Enough already

You've been much too kind
We can't go on like this forever

# The Ghost of Joice Heth on the Truth and the Trees

The truth is worth a lot. There is no doubt
about that. As George Washington's father said,
"the truth is worth more than a thousand trees,
though blossomed with silver, and their fruits
the purest gold." I picked fruit
for my plantation owners. I picked fruit
before I met a man who allowed me
to lie. The fruit was worth a lot. I stole
apples and pears and gave them to my children
who were sick and dying. Our babies
sick and waiting to be set free.
The truth is not freedom. No doubt
freedom is a lie when I watched my children
who were slaves (as I was a slave)
enjoy their fruit a bit too heartily. I did not
eat my fruit. That is why I became so thin.
I wanted the truth to nourish me. When I began
to tell lies, I left the plantation and my children
and lived for a while in a forest full of trees.
It was so full of trees, you couldn't move
without knocking into one. It was so full
of trees, I mistook myself for one, my feet
planted on the ground, my arms
outstretched over my head. The trees didn't seem
to mind. They liked the company. But I felt bad
that I couldn't leave nature
alone. I apologized to the trees for ruining
their bark, I apologized to the birds for interrupting
their songs. I was a noisy woman
who told noisy lies. The trees were blossomed
with silver. I stole the metal, kept it in my apron.
The metal became the truth for me. It shined
so bright that I didn't think it could be anything else.
Little did I know. Little did I know so much in the world
shines brightly.

# The Aesthetics of the Damned

Satan sported new threads. Lime green leisure suit
and black patent leather shoes. His lascivious smile

looked less menacing than the grin of a professor
who harasses his slow students.

A small piece of human flesh was caught
between his front two teeth. I decided

not to mention it. He smelled like strawberry lotion.
It concerned me. What happened to the lovely scent

of gasoline crossed with damp armpit hair?
You could get high on the odor. Ten years ago

I had chanted His name in a public bathroom.
Within seconds he arrived, dressed in well-ironed khakis

and a pink Polo shirt, eager to take my soul.
My girlfriend Cindy had left me

for no one in particular. She wanted to volunteer
more time at the Salvation Army Thrift Store, helping

people look their best on a ten dollar budget.
I told Him the story. He looked bored

and disappeared in a cloud of smoke.
Something horrible had happened since then.

Satan and I sat on a park bench in the forest preserve,
tossing bread crumbs to the needy pigeons, making fun

of the bench-ridden old men who wore unshapely turtlenecks.
"You don't look so good," I said. He twirled

his tail around his forefinger and said,
"Things haven't been good lately.

God may be able to reinvent himself more times than Madonna.
He has infinite resources. I have a stricter budget."

I brushed back his bangs and held him in my arms.
He sobbed a little. God seemed so lucky.

How did it feel to not ever have to worry
about your appearance? Fresh air and sunlight

and the sweet sight of doves never go
out of style. Martyrs and saints wear dull, plain sheets

to match their dull, virtuous lives. To sin with success
you need to be careful not to draw too much attention

to yourself for the wrong reasons. The maniacs who pour poison
into Tylenol capsules and then put the fatal packages

back on the store shelves don jeans and t-shirts
with odd logos: "Give Death a Chance." The lack

of hierarchies in Heaven reportedly causes a lot
of infighting, snobby cliques. Hell revels in pretensions.

Appearances matter. You can't move from the Eighth
Circle of Hell to the Third without gaining the required

sixty seven pounds and having a fair amount
of blood on your hands. The Devil may wear a tweed jacket

and corduroys in the summer months. His hunchbacked henchmen
may gargle with human blood, spit up all over themselves,

refuse to wipe their faces clean. We humans must fashion
our fashions sensibly. Who hasn't shoplifted

a navy blue skirt to match the bruise on their forehead
they got from running into a lamppost

on their way to a Lord & Taylor Clearance Sale?
Less than a day later you may try to exchange

that outfit for a cheap pair of pantyhose
and a pair of earrings more appropriate

for a Christmas tree than your face. But still.
The shame we feel as we jog back to the store

will make it all worthwhile. Only the dead
like to sit still. Only God likes us unadorned, unadored.

# CLEARING THE AIR

Forgive me for refusing to believe
the world was dying
inside your body.

Forgive me for the time I lit a peach
scented candle inside my bedroom and waited for you to pound
on my door and say, "My own son is trying to smoke me out of my house."
Forgive me for hating you when you beat my father with your bare hands
after you sniffed his jacket and smelled cigarettes. Once I caught him
chain smoking in the backyard garden, burying

the butts underneath the petunias and crocuses. He promised me
that he'd buy you a Service Merchandise humidifier
and a dozen long-stem roses as an apology for the sins you never knew he
    committed. Forgive me for complaining about the sterility of the air
    in our house. I claimed
the mist was obliterating my brain cells, making it impossible
for me to receive higher than a 1.6 semester GPA. Forgive me for
    mocking you
in front of my friends when you offered them purified water
and organic sesame crackers as an afterschool snack. I remember once

you coming home exhausted from teaching kindergarten
and not being able to leave your bed for two and a half days.
You asked me to call in sick for you and we both laughed
when I told you they asked if you had a drinking problem.
This is the truth: I wish you did guzzle vodka every morning
with your numerous herbs and homeopathies. Why not die from something
everyone believes in? Like cancer or AIDS or heart disease. I remember
you and eight other women meeting in our living room, reading
Native American poetry aloud, talking about an Oregon tribe

with no live births in the past five years. You seemed to know
facts about pesticides, chemicals, and uranium in greater detail
than your own families, children. When the doctors diagnosed you

with a secondary condition called fibromyalgia, I boasted
to my friends you were suffering from something
with a name. Forgive me for shoveling dirt into your grave,
imagining the broken earth crushing your body, breaking
your bones, filling you with a happiness you never found with me.

# I Don't Want My Life Back

A year after the senior class voted
my older brother Most Likely
To Die From a Heart Attack,

a neighbor spotted him on a streetcorner,
passing out religious pamphlets
to ungrateful jaywalkers.

Slumped in the front seats
of our station wagon, Mother and I watched him
approach old ladies and junkies

with the same calm grace. He never looked
happier. We knew we had to save him.
I missed him stomping around the house,

cursing when the people from upstairs
played their music too loud,
making it impossible for him to concentrate

and complete the extra credit
he didn't need for his accounting class.
For his Stanford interview, he bought

a navy blue sport coat and then twirled
around in our living room, waiting
for an applause. Our alleged lack

of enthusiasm convinced him to purchase
a whole new green linen suit, cufflinks.
We were surprised he didn't get a haircut.

At least a trim. His worries always made us
forget we didn't have a father to lord
over us. Now with the sunlight spotlighting

my brother's bald head, Mother and I devised a plan.
The cult deprogrammers didn't offer any money back
guarantees. You took your chances. Six hundred

a day. Plus expenses. "He gave them
his college tuition," Mother said to the two men.
They plotted to kidnap my brother,

dragging him to a Motel Six
until they "reverse brainwashed" him.
I stayed in the motel room and waited.

I imagined them asking my brother questions
as Mother drove the van onto the curb, waiting
for them to seize his arms and shove him into the back,

tying him up, stuffing a gag into his mouth.
"Don't speed," one of the hired help would say, "We're in no rush."
He wouldn't understand. Cruising through stoplights,

Mother would step on the gas. We had both fantasized
about my brother returning to our kitchen table,
crying over a B+, claiming his life was over,

grad school nothing more than a silly fantasy.
His forehead bloodied, his arms bruised,
my brother was strapped to the motel's twin bed

with Father's old leather belts, rope.
We paid the men their fees and told them
to leave. "We got our money's worth," Mother said.

My brother spit in our faces, swearing he'd never join
our family again. We didn't care.
We tightened the belts and rope,

read aloud xeroxed newspaper
articles exposing the cult's lies.
"So?" he said. "I don't want my life back."

I slugged him. Mother bit her lip so hard it bled.
Someone banged their fist on the adjacent wall.
We dropped to our knees and whispered our pleas.

"Please don't resist," we chanted. "Be with us."

# CRITICISM

Twelve years old. The first thing I read
in the *Daily Voice* were the movie reviews. Nothing excited me
more than seeing *Toxic Avenger* receive zero
stars (out of the possible four). The critic labeled the film
"vitally stupid. An insult to the human race."
The film was about a suicidal high school geek who throws
himself into a bubbling vat of acid, transforming himself
into a self-righteous superhero who disfigures beautiful cheerleaders.
"Dull misogyny" was another jab. How relieved I was
that something deemed so unnecessary
could receive attention. I read that review
at least seventy-six times as my parents planned
their trip to Cancun without me. When I booed a puppet show,
complaining the animals looked too human,
my teacher sat me in the corner of the classroom
facing the wall and forced me to write
an apology, complimenting the troupe's dumb socks and whiny voices.
I scissored reviews of any sort from the newspaper,
memorized the headline and opening sentence,
and then snuck into the upstairs attic where I unearthed
family photo albums and substituted pictures
of my parents with the succinct critiques:
*How many more movies can anyone stomach about domestic violence,*
*dull adulteries? These days everyone wallows*
*in their own pain. The world needs to cheer up.* My father said marriage
was the worst mistake he made other than
having a son. I eventually got angry enough
to throw a tantrum and a kitchen appliance.
Our fights were earnest and woefully uninspired.
I watched Siskel and Ebert's TV show
and cheered when they turned their thumbs down. I imagined
the fledgling director calling his wife,
begging her to leave Hollywood with him and join
the Peace Corps, somewhere in the Himalayas
or a strange island with unphotogenic natives. No doubt their bodies

reeked of popcorn and other peoples' pathos. I lost
weight and even ran away from home once,
standing on the edge of the highway,
thumb raised in the air. No one stopped.
When I watched Saturday morning cartoons
without commenting, my parents doled out Hershey's
chocolate kisses and money for my college fund. "Don't depend
so heavily on secondary sources," my freshman
English teacher said, "Trust the primary ones."
Not until grad school did I finish reading
a novel in its entirety. Back covers
obsessed me. I read and re-read the blurbs,
memorizing the praise of strangers,
hoping and fearing other networks existed.
Clutching felt tip markers, I diagrammed
the connections on construction paper, linking authors
and critics to agents and publishers in order
to construct something resembling a family tree.
After I finished, I mocked the crooked lines, bloated
cursive, ugly use of color. No way would I
have magnetized my own illustration
to the refrigerator in the kitchen where my parents'
friends waited for a stiffer drink and livelier music.
But who could blame them for looking
at the drawing and mistaking its flaws
as the imaginative risks of a child?

# THE TOMB OF EVE

*For several decades in the late-19th and early-20th century,*
*thousands of Muslims trekked to a cemetery near Jedda, Arabia,*
*to seek the advice of a woman who claimed to be Eve.*

At the Tomb of Eve,
there is a booth
where you put a coin
in a slot and ask the Mother
of Mankind a question
through a tube. The men in line
squint, try to see through the curtains
which reveal nothing more
than a profile of an unremarkable
woman: slender nose, long, thin
neck, perhaps a bald head.
She never moves, stunned
by the predictability
of the questions. "Do you think
Adam would be considered
a good catch these days?" you want
to ask. But instead you say,
"Does God truly forgive us for our sins?"
She sighs and then says
nothing. For the first time
you want to believe
this Eve is a normal woman,
divorced, stuck with a kid.
This is her part time job. You imagine
her sitting on a bench inside the booth.
She's filing her nails, combing her girl's hair
as she half-listens to you ask,
"Was it really worth it?"
Her kid begins to cry, says she wants
to go home. Eve doesn't hear
you repeat yourself

for the third time. She's thinking
about everything she needs to do:
laundry, carpool, housecleaning, meeting
her lover who never seems tempted
in the least to leave his wife.
"So was it worth it?" you ask.
"Every penny," she mumbles
a moment after another coin falls
into her girl's palm.

# BLIND DATE WITH CAVAFY

This much I remember:
he overtipped the waiter.
Our conversation always changed

from religion and history
to his favorite gym and dance clubs
when the waiter refilled

waterglasses at a nearby table
or brought us another course of our meal.
Cavafy couldn't keep his eyes

on me or his dinner salad.
He kept stabbing the tablecloth,
finally ripping a hole in the fabric.

Whenever I needed a condiment,
he volunteered to get the waiter's attention.
I want to remember him

as a man who didn't need
to be facing the front door
to see who came in,

at least when he was with me.
The only thing I knew before the date:
he wrote love poems in cafes.

I read him a few lines
I composed during the advent of our meeting.
"Creating is better

than not creating," he said.
I took it as a compliment.
"Unbutton you collar," he said,

offering me a spoonful of his dessert.
"Your chest hair needs to breath."
He asked the waiter for the check

and the name of the cologne he was wearing.
"I'm not wearing any," the waiter said.
"Interesting," Cavafy said.

Halfway to my house,
he said he forgot his wallet
on our table. "I should go back

and get it," he said. "Next week
I'll come over." I don't remember what happened
the next week. Or the week

after that. Except that I saw
a book of his poems in a library.
The descriptions of the men

are basically all the same. Then again,
how many ways are there
to describe a man? How many men

are worthy of a memory? I never read
a poem of his through to the end. I want
to believe he left something, someone out.

# In Praise of Hype

Praise radio WXRZ movie critic
Susan Edmonds for praising
every movie she's ever seen.
Praise her for always being
the first in line with a line
for the ad campaign of a new movie.
How can you not admire
someone who claims to have seen
"the film of the decade"
three times in one week? How can you
not love someone whose idea
of faint praise is a "rollicking
tour de force?" I imagine
sitting next to Susan
in a dark theatre, straining
my eyes to read the scribbles
on her paper. They are
the firm, unhesitant markings
of a fan. Every word seems
to be followed by a parade
of exclamation marks. I imagine
scanning her notebook, finding
the same sentence written
about every movie: "Triple A-plus!"
No details about the plot, no
character names, no notes
of irritation or specific joys. I imagine
she never stays for the ending
credits. She doesn't want
to know the names of those
she claims to love. She always
imagines movie directors scanning
the newspaper ads, lingering
over her blurbs, as if they were secret
valentines. As if they were written
for something other than
a special occasion.

# CONSIDER THE FATES

Because Mom failed to leave a honey-cake
outside a cave on one of the eastern spurs
of Taygetus, I will not be guaranteed
a successful life, one full of dull, easy victories:
winning $137.86 in the Illinois Daily Lotto, working
as a Kinney's shoe salesman or Commonwealth Edison
meter reader for minimum wage, marrying someone
with an adequate IQ and all their appendages intact.
Mom tried to read the raised moles and other strange
marks on my forehead in order to estimate the degree
and intensity of my tragic flaw. On the Richter scale,
it'd receive at least a 7. Give or take a point.
Only one problem exists. We haven't figured out
what the flaw is. She's narrowed it down to slothfulness,
good, old-fashioned misogyny, and a predictable
youthful impulsiveness. "Don't use psychology
as a scapegoat for your mental instability," my shrink said,
"Consider the fates as an explanation of your fear of being drafted
in the next world war or choking to death
on a communion wafer." I never saw him after that.
Months later his office closed. I consulted my aunt
for wisdom: Was it true the Fates were present at the birth
of Athena from the head of Zeus? Could it be
not even Zeus was exempt from their decree?
"No one is ever safe," she said. Maybe.
But if danger is inevitable, let's throw a hootenanny,
celebrating the agents of our own destruction. To take full credit
for our own demise is egotistical and woefully unfashionable.
Blame your father for failing to attend
your first grade talent show. Everyone commented
on how well you manipulated the argyle sock
with the crocodile face. You never did feel
any desire to enter show business after that. Blame
your poor treatment of women on your sister's high school
boyfriend, who ditched her on Prom Night.
Blame the garbage man for picking up the trash

after three. If he had done it earlier, your family wouldn't have found
your bank receipts. Which revealed a zero balance. You gambled
your entire inheritance away at the racetrack
in one Sunday afternoon. Don't worry about anybody else's
shame and guilt. A mortal's favorite pasttime is denial. But the Fates,
those old women: They're a different story. They'll want
you to create a scroll of their injustices against you. Perhaps
even laminate it. Hang it on a statue
in front of City Hall. Whisper their evils
in the ear of a pilot. If he doesn't skywrite
their nasty forebodings in proper alphabetical order
above your dreamboat's house, they'll promise to take
his wife's life. Would they make good on the threat?
Who knows? Except them. And why should they tell us?
The Fates will live forever. Whatever joy they receive
from the looks of jealousy and shock on our faces when our younger
    brother
wins a Nobel prize or dies under the feet of a flock
of stampeding ostriches is well-deserved. They have more lives
to organize than a cruise director. Not to mention they can't depend
on a staff of underpaid inferior interns. Humans need direction
and urgency as much as all-you-can eat salad bars and endless
games of shuffleboard. But we'll pretend otherwise. We'll lean back
in our pink plastic lawn chairs and pretend mosquitoes are sucking
our skin when we know full well that Clotho was sitting on a cloud,
fiddling with the spindle and dropped the thread.
Which now grazes the flesh and begs its full, necessary attention.
An itch and a scratch is only the beginning.

# SYNESTHESIA

My brother tasted shapes. McDonald's hamburgers
were most wonderful parallelograms.
The Rice Krispie treats never had quite enough
perpendicularity. But Caesar salad,
oh Caesar salad! You would never devour
a more delicious bounty of line segments.
Meatloaf and green beans disappeared from my brother's plate so quick
it was like magic. Once something got caught
in my brother's windpipe. The lunchroom aid slapped
his back. A small hunk of tuna flew
through the air. All the kids clapped. Two periods later
I heard the story: "Your brother almost died." My response:
"Too bad." When they saw him in the hallway, they patted
his shoulder and said, "Congratulations." As if he'd won
the spelling bee for the seventh year in a row. Everyone wanted
to become his friend. He was a living good luck charm
and he described things in funny ways. They begged
him to come for dinner and grace their meals.
He accepted their invitations and complimented
the dull American dishes. *This tuna casserole is*
*an inspired rhombus. Can I have another glass*
*of pink lemonade? It tastes perfectly*
*sharp.* Parents loved him. He inspired
their kids to see leftovers in a new way. Or maybe
he excited them so much about their meals
there never was any extra to pack away
in Tupperware bowls for tomorrow. I don't know.
I was never invited. And I never asked
too many questions. What interested me was
the potentiality of death. My brother said, "Death is
like that robin you saw yesterday lying in the middle of the street
that was so gone it came back to life." I looked a little confused
so he added: "Or remember when we were swinging
so high in the air, we thought for sure we'd catapult
our own bodies across the playground and crash

into the metal bars of the jungle gym. It's like that. Except
you're never expecting the fall. And when you do,
it's on top of a trampoline as large as the universe.
Your soul bounces for at least two eternities." Death sounded
like a pleasant change of pace. From my life. Which consisted
of girls asking my brother what it felt like to kiss them
("Like the sun shining through stained glass
after a monsoon on a Sunday afternoon"); friends begging him
to be ruthless about their new hairdos ("The perfect cross
between the smell of burnt tapioca pudding and undercooked
pot roast"); Mother wanting a critique of her latest strapless dress,
("The sound of a waterfall doing the jitterbug with a harem of robins").
One day after shoving my fingers into my ears and shutting my eyes,
I walked into traffic. My body went numb and I fainted.
Next thing I know a police office asked, "You're young.
You can be anything you want. Why roadkill?"
I went home and did nothing for weeks.
Death still eluded me. But life became more clear.
It's like being clad in a straightjacket and bowtie
and having to crawl toward a hidden door in a room
as large as a baseball stadium and as dark as the scream
from someone's throat. That someone is you. Don't yell
too hard. You may wake up and realize life
isn't like that. It isn't really like anything.
But life does like itself and it needs you.

# How I Tried to Banish Self-Insight and Knowledge from My Life and the World

One day I decided interesting things
no longer interested me. I forfeited every game
of Trivial Pursuit. I used Sunday newspapers
as bath mats. Reading a book from cover to cover
was a long-term commitment, limiting me
in its monogamous demand. Making up pet names
for my sleeping pills occupied one Friday night.
Another time I broke into the payroll office
of the Urbana Public Library and stole an employee list.
For three hours, I called every person and demanded
they quit their jobs or else their houses would be burned.
Everyone obeyed. The library was forced
to close down for 23 days. During that time
I invited Knowledge over for a dinner party.
Knowledge was a blue-eyed dwarf dressed in overalls
and a tiara. We sat in a locked steel vault, drinking pink
lemonade and nibbling graham crackers. We chatted
about nothing. Hours later I confessed to not committing
the combination to memory. I swallowed
the slip of paper and then said, "We'll never see
a shopping mall information center or daylight again."
For months our lives were a pleasant celebration
of non-existence. We peed in Fruitopia bottles
and then twisted the caps back on. "Do you feel
like you're missing out on something?" Knowledge asked.
As if I decided to ditch my senior prom and go
to a Sox game. I refused
to think. Self-reflection felt as dumb
as eating a main meal with a dessert fork.
Putting my arms around Knowledge, our cold cheeks brushed,
our nipples hardened. I smelled the dead
weight of facts and remembered the first two
numbers of the combination.

# About the Author

Steve Fellner was born and raised in Chicago, and currently is an Assistant Professor of English at SUNY Brockport. His poems and essays have appeared in *Doubletake, North American Review, Northwest Review, Mid-American Review, Puerto del Sol, The Sun,* among others. He attended University of Illinois at Urbana-Champaign, Syracuse University, University of Alabama, and received his Ph.D. from the University of Utah. *Blind Date with Cavafy* is his first book of poems and was chosen by Denise Duhamel as the winner of the 2006 Marsh Hawk Press Poetry Prize. He is also finishing a memoir entitled *Where I Went Wrong.*

Claudia Carlson, *The Elephant House*
Steve Fellner, *Blind Date with Cavafy*
Basil King, *77 Beasts: Basil King's Bestiary*
Rochelle Ratner, *Balancing Acts*
Corinne Robins, *Today's Menu*
Mary Mackey, *Breaking the Fever*
Sigman Byrd, *Under the Wanderer's Star*
Ed Foster, *What He Ought To Know*
Sharon Olinka, *The Good City*
Harriet Zinnes, *Whither Nonstopping*
Sandy McIntosh, *The After-Death History of My Mother*
Eileen R. Tabios, *I Take Thee English for My Beloved*
Burt Kimmelman, *Somehow*
Stephen Paul Miller, *Skinny Eighth Avenue*
Jacquelyn Pope, *Watermark*
Jane Augustine, *Night Lights*
Thomas Fink, *After Taxes*
Martha King, *Imperfect Fit*
Susan Terris, *Natural Defenses*
Daniel Morris, *Bryce Passage*
Corinne Robins, *One Thousand Years*
Chard deNiord, *Sharp Golden Thorn*
Rochelle Ratner, *House and Home*
Basil King, *Mirage*
Sharon Dolin, *Serious Pink*
Madeline Tiger, *Birds of Sorrow and Joy*
Patricia Carlin, *Original Green*
Stephen Paul Miller, *The Bee Flies in May*
Edward Foster, *MAHREM: Things Men Should Do for Men*
Eileen Tabios, *Reproductions of the Empty Flagpole*
Harriet Zinnes, *Drawing on the Wall*
Thomas Fink, *Gossip: A Book of Poems*
Jane Augustine, *Arbor Vitae*
Sandy McIntosh, *Between Earth and Sky*
Burt Kimmelman and Fred Caruso, *The Pond at Cape May Point*

Marsh Hawk Press is a juried collective committed to publishing poetry, especially to poetry with an affinity to the visual arts.

Artistic Advisory Board: Toi Derricotte, Denise Duhamel, Marilyn Hacker, Allan Kornblum, Maria Mazzioti Gillan, Alicia Ostriker, David Shapiro, Nathaniel Tarn, Anne Waldman, and John Yau.

For more information, please go to: http://www.marshhawkpress.org.